RAYMOND BIAL
Portrait of a Farm Family

HOUGHTON MIFFLIN COMPANY   BOSTON   1995

Acknowledgments

I would like to thank Audrey Bryant, Amy Bernstein, and the other talented staff at Houghton Mifflin for their efforts on behalf of *Portrait of a Farm Family*. I would also like to thank the Steidingers who welcomed me into their home and Shawna Adams who introduced me to this wonderful family.

Copyright © 1995 by Raymond Bial

Library of Congress Cataloging-in-Publication Data
Bial, Raymond.
Portrait of a farm family / written and photo illustrated by Raymond Bial.
    p. cm.
  ISBN 0-395-69936-3
    1. Farm life — Illinois — Fairbury Region — Juvenile literature. 2. Family farms — Illinois — Fairbury Region — Juvenile literature. 3. Dairy farming — Illinois — Fairbury Region — Juvenile literature. 4. Steidinger family — Juvenile literature. [1. Farm life.] I. Title.
S519.B53 1995   94-38201
338.1'0973 — dc20   CIP
                                                    AC

Printed in Singapore

TWP 10 9 8 7 6 5 4 3 2 1

Portrait of a Farm Family is dedicated to the Steidinger family, who cheerfully welcomed me into their home, and to my six-year-old daughter, Sarah, who accompanied me on some visits and, camera in hand, photographed right alongside me.

*"Those who labor in the earth are the chosen people of God,
if He ever had a chosen people..."*

—THOMAS JEFFERSON

FIVE A.M. Mark Steidinger climbs out of bed and gets dressed. Wiping sleep from his eyes and yawning deeply, the thirteen-year-old trudges out of the house and across the yard to collect the Holstein cows that make up his family's dairy herd. A trace of haze lingers near the ground as he approaches the cows.

To the east, the circle of the sun edges over a neighbor's farm about a mile away, firing the sky with a blend of yellow, orange, and rose. However, Mark and his father, Dennis Steidinger, who is already heading to the barn, scarcely have time to glance at the new day breaking over the fields. Low and somber, a cow calls as Mark slides open the barn door that leads to the milking parlor and his father flicks on the lights.

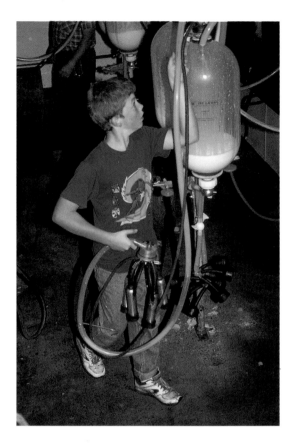

In the old days, using portable machines, milking took twice as long as it does now. It takes about an hour to milk the cows, each of which gives more than fifty pounds (more than six gallons) of milk a day.

Mark ushers the first eight cows into the milking parlor, a concrete-floored room in the barn that's filled with an assortment of milking equipment. The gawky animals are guided into metal stalls called stanchions. To keep the animals content while they're milked, grain is delivered automatically to a trough in front of the stanchions. While the cows are eating, Dennis washes the turgid udders with disinfectant and slips the sockets of the automatic milking machine onto the teats of the black and white cows. Rich, creamy milk begins to surge through the clear plastic tubes into large bottles, where the exact amount of milk each cow gives is recorded. This tells Dennis if a cow isn't giving as much milk as she should. The milk then flows into a refrigerated tank.

This automated system makes milking more efficient — you need only two people to milk fifty-five cows instead of five or six. It's also safer because the milk is never exposed to possible contamination. Every other day a Prairie Farms Dairy truck swings into the yard and pumps the milk from the stainless steel cooling tank, after which the tank is cleaned out for the next milking.

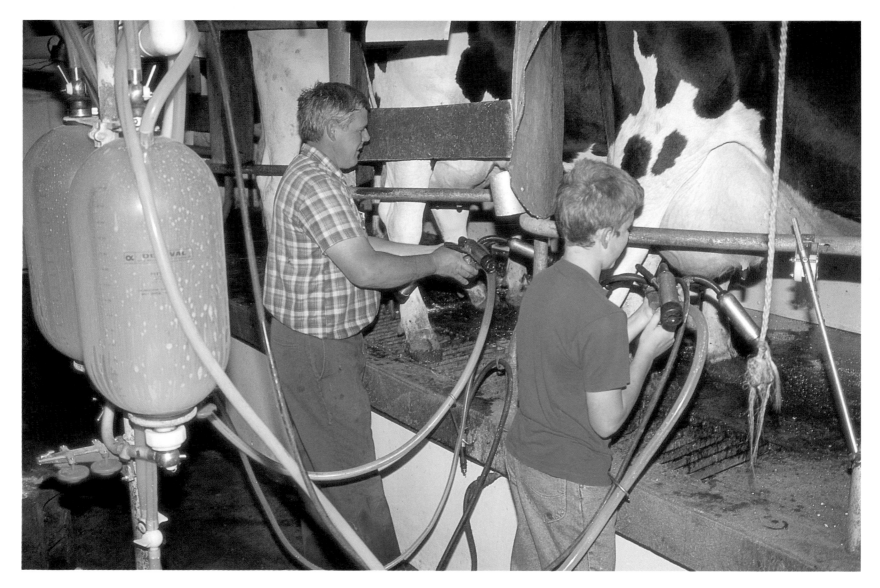

Each cow consumes roughly eighteen pounds of grain, thirty pounds of silage, eight pounds of hay, and twenty to twenty-five gallons of water a day.

These heifers will be bred when they are fifteen months old and weigh about 850 pounds. They have their first calves nine months later.

On their farm near Fairbury, Illinois, the Steidingers keep a herd of about fifty-five Holstein cows. The farm is primarily a dairy operation, though crops are grown to supplement the income from the milk. The cows must be milked every morning and every evening, seven days a week. Dennis always rises before dawn to do the milking, while Mark takes turns helping with two of his older brothers: twenty-one-year-old Phil, who's taking over the dairy operation from their father, and sixteen-year-old Tim.

Dennis and Phil breed the cows every year. A cow will give milk for ten months, after which she is allowed to go dry to build up her strength before she has another calf. Most cows will be productive for six or seven years, but a good cow may produce calves and milk for eleven or twelve years.

Rambo acquired her name from her father. The Steidinger cows are artificially inseminated because Dennis doesn't want to keep a bull. "Bulls are dangerous," he says, "and we have small children." Once Rambo has had a calf she'll join the milk herd.

9

Although they consume larger quantities of feed, Dennis prefers Holsteins because they give considerably more milk than other breeds of cows. Milk production is measured in pounds (roughly 8.6 pounds to the gallon) and butterfat content. The price the Steidingers receive for their milk varies from week to week, but even a change of a few cents per pound can make the difference between losing money and making a profit. Like other farmers, the Steidingers are at the mercy of fluctuating prices. "We never know from one week to the next what price we're going to get for our milk," Dennis says. "Sometimes it's pretty hard to just cover expenses."

Because of declining milk prices, dairy farms across the United States—most of them family-owned—are going out of business. Once considered "America's Dairyland," Wisconsin, for example, is currently losing nearly 10 percent of its dairy farms each year. Ironically, farmers have become so efficient over the years that an oversupply of milk has kept prices low, so low that they often drop below the cost of production. And of all the people involved in the production, processing, and delivery of milk, cheese, and other dairy products, the farmers who supply the milk receive the smallest share of the income. This is true of most farmers: the amount of money a farmer receives for the wheat in a loaf of bread, for instance, is less than the cost of the wrapper.

These fifty acres of corn will be ready to be cut for silage by the end of August and the resulting nine hundred tons of silage will be stored in the farm's towering silos. In addition to the silage, the cattle also consume about six thousand bushels of corn and four thousand bales of hay each year.

Although their main job is to control the rodent population on the farm, the cats welcome milk as a break from a steady diet of field mice and table scraps.

It takes about an hour to milk the cows on the Steidinger farm, after which they're let back into the barnyard and Mark continues with his other morning chores. First, he pours a little milk into dishes for the twenty cats that patrol the barn and other outbuildings on the farm where grain is stored.

Mark doesn't mind chores; he even tends to like them, "except milking." Here he's drawing whole milk and bottlefeeding a newborn calf.

While Dennis cleans up the milking parlor, Mark fills milk bottles for the newborn calves and handfeeds them in the pens at the back of the farmyard. Mark also mixes a powdered formula called "milk replacer" — it's less expensive and just as nutritious as whole milk — in buckets and feeds this "instant milk" to the older calves.

After birth, a calf is moved into one of the calf pens. For the first few days it is bottle-fed its mother's milk, which is rich in colostrum — a yellowish fluid with minerals and antibodies that help the calf get off to a healthy start.

Instead of milking, "Mark loves to drive the tractor, especially in the fields," Dennis says. "His favorite is hauling beans and corn from the fields to the bins."

Tim pours fresh water for one of the calves kept in the pens behind the barn. In addition to his many chores on the farm he also works part-time for a hog farmer down the road.

"To me, farm life is lots of work and early morning hours," Tim says.

Tim shows up next to fill buckets with well water for the older calves that are now eating grain, hay, and silage (a mixture of cornstalks, shucks, and unripened ears) and no longer need the milk formula. The milk cows have a ready supply of fresh water in troughs located in each of the large pens called feedlots that are set up next to the barns.

To add to their income from milk, the Steidingers also feed out, or raise for beef, the bull calves born on their farm. Once they reach a certain weight, they'll be sold to neighbors or taken to a local auction. All of the female calves, or heifers, are kept for the milk herd.

Bull calves are fed out until they're about eighteen months old. Roughly a fifth of the Steidingers' income is earned from calves raised for beef, and with most of the fifty-five cows producing a calf each year there are always nearly as many calves in the feedlots.

After milking, it's time to feed the cows. Phil arrives, slides into the tractor seat, and drives the vehicle and wagon to the silo where he loads silage into the wagon. Chugging along on the tractor, Phil pulls the load of silage back to the feedlot where it is automatically poured into a concrete trough as the tractor rolls along the edge of the fence.

Phil is preparing to someday take charge of the farm. "Farming's a good learning experience," he says. "And you can be your own boss. You can pretty much do what you want from day to day as long as the work gets done."

Phil loads the wagon with a conveyor, a machine that pushes silage from the silo through a tube into the wagon. Silage, a mix of corn stalks, leaves, and unripened ears, is stored in the silo to ferment, or age, giving it a flavor irresistible to cows.

As Phil eases the tractor forward, silage is evenly poured into the concrete trough, insuring that each animal will get its share.

Although they haven't invested in a lot of expensive equipment, the Steidingers have automated their dairy operation. Equipment such as automatic milking machines and tractors enables a relatively small number of people to do a large amount of work. A farm the size of the Steidingers' would, in the past, have taken twice as much labor. Before Dennis automated the farm he could handle only about twenty-four cows, which were milked with a portable machine. Now the work is handily done by their family.

Problems can arise, however, with buying too much expensive equipment; the payments can create too much overhead (the money needed to pay bills). The Steidingers have carefully considered each purchase, weighing the benefits of automation to keep competitive against the expense of the equipment.

"I want to be a farmer," Phil says, "because, if I ever have a family, the country's a good place to raise children. Sure, milk prices go up and down, but if you're a hard worker, things work out. You'll never get rich, but money's not everything."

17

Much of the heavy work on the farm must be done with machinery. Here Mark and Phil hook a chain around a large bale of hay. The hay will be lifted by the front-end loader of the tractor and dropped into a feeder.

Along with silage, cows eat both hay and grain, and this morning the hay feeder needs to be reloaded. Phil attaches a front-end loader to the tractor and picks up a large round bale, which he maneuvers overhead and dumps into the feeder.

In the evening, the Steidingers repeat each of these chores, milking at "five and five," seven days a week. Sometimes Mark handles the evening milking by himself if his parents go out. Chores can become tedious, but they have to be done.

Once the cattle are milked, fed, and watered, Dennis and his sons walk back to the house where Jane Steidinger has breakfast waiting for them. In addition to their battalion of cats, they have a mixed collie dog named Sable and a flock of white leghorn chickens. Leghorns are smaller than other breeds, but consistently lay more eggs. Until recently, they also had a pet raccoon, but it has since wandered off to parts unknown.

Farmers must invest in a considerable amount of equipment to plow, plant, and harvest their crops, as well as to work around the barnyard. While not the most expensive pieces of equipment, a front-end loader and tractor like this one still costs thousands of dollars.

	Number of farms (thousands)	Average farm size (acres)
1980	2,439	426
1981	2,439	424
1982	2,406	427
1983	2,378	430
1984	2,333	436
1985	2,292	441
1986	2,249	447
1987	2,212	451
1988	2,197	453
1989	2,170	457
1990	2,140	461
1991	2,105	467
1992	2,095	468

(Source: National Agricultural Statistics Services)

This chart shows the steady decline in the number of American farms and the increase in the size of the remaining farms in recent years.

Like other farm families, the Steidingers face financial challenges. Several years ago, reports of family farms going bankrupt became alarmingly common. Attempts have since been made to insure the survival of the family farm, yet each year the number of farms in the United States declines, while the average farm size increases. These larger farms, sometimes called "agribusinesses," are often owned by corporations or rented to farmers by absentee landlords. Many farmers feel it's necessary to expand the size of their farms and invest heavily in expensive equipment to compete with agribusinesses. "Get big or get out" is a popular saying.

Many people believe that the days of the family farm have passed. If so, the rural landscape will look very different from this scene in which the Steidinger farm is visible in the distance.

The Steidinger family includes (left to right) Matt (18), Dennis, Phil, Jane, Mike (22), who lives in town, Hope (10), Mark, Tim, Faith (1), Joy (19), and her new husband, Jason Kilgus. "Many hands make light work," Jane says.

Mark drives the tractor while Phil stacks bales of hay late into the evening. The Steidingers are succeeding by diversity; in addition to growing corn and hay for feed they also raise a small "cash crop"— this year it's soybeans, which they combine soon after harvesting the silage corn.

Livestock operations raising beef cattle, dairy cattle, hogs, sheep, or poultry make up the remaining specialized farms. Often grain crops are grown on these farms to feed the livestock and pasture may be provided for grazing sheep and cattle. But despite the large percentage of specialized farms, there is a growing realization that there is not a single best way to farm. Approaches vary and are often heatedly debated.

Monoculture requires large amounts of chemicals, both fertilizers and pesticides, to maintain productivity. This is risky; it can be safer to vary the farm's products. For instance, if prices are down for one crop, they may just as likely be up for another raised on the same farm. On a practical level, many farmers simply cannot afford the cost of a large farm and opt for a smaller, more varied operation. Others look for ways to add to their income, often working long hours and taking a second job off the farm. Large or small, farmers know that their income must exceed their expenses, or they won't be farming for long.

The survival of family farms is further complicated by the consolidation of the food industry into huge corporate enterprises that control every stage of a crop from planting to delivery onto grocery shelves. These corporations often own farms or contract to buy only from large agribusinesses. This makes it difficult for small farms to compete. Farming has always been a continuing process of innovation, but the twentieth century has brought unparalleled technological changes that must be addressed by the Steidingers and other families across the country if they are to keep their farms.

In addition to careful automation and use of the available land, the Steidingers have made the decision to keep their farm self-sufficient, never taking on more than they can do themselves. Along with daily chores, the brothers and sisters also help their parents take care of the crops, muck out the barn, repair equipment, and generally pitch in wherever needed. During the school year they rise early, often at 5:00 A.M., finish chores by 6:30, come in for breakfast by 7:00, and catch the school bus out by the mailbox at 7:20. In the evening they have to balance chores and schoolwork.

Whether mucking out the barn or mending fences, boots come in handy, especially when a good rain turns the feedlots into mud. When not in use, the boots are strewn in the yard to dry off in the sun.

The Steidingers do not use any of their land as pasture for their cows because they don't have a lot of extra acreage, and the velvety black soil of their farm is too valuable for growing grain crops.

The Steidingers' farm is about 240 acres, which is smaller than most in America; the average U.S. farm is about double that size. The Steidingers have decided to stay relatively small. Their acreage supports the dairy herd, as well as about eighty acres of soybeans or field corn, which is grown not as livestock feed but as a cash crop for additional income. The rest of the land is given over to hay and corn to feed their cattle.

The Steidingers try to be self-sufficient. Along with eggs and meat, the farm provides much of the fruit and vegetables for the family. Sometimes they swap vegetables for sweetcorn, peaches, and other produce that friends, relatives, and neighbors have in abundance. Like many farm women, Jane puts in a sizable vegetable garden next to the house.

Jane and the girls brighten the yard with flowers grown at the edge of the vegetable garden, picking the flowers to make bouquets and to adorn the table at dinner. This offers Jane a welcome break from canning, one of the most formidable and time-consuming tasks of the farm.

Hope helps her mother with the garden. Faith also picks an occasional cherry tomato — and just about any other vegetable she can get her hands on. As part of their garden work, Jane and Hope also have to keep an eye on her.

Each summer, Jane cans one hundred quarts of applesauce, seventy quarts each of peaches, pears, green beans, and tomatoes, forty quarts of spinach, thirty quarts of plums, twenty-five quarts of beets, and many pints of jams and jellies.

Canning season always falls in the hottest months of the year, when one would rather be almost any place other than by a heated stove in a steam-filled kitchen. But come winter, the jars of peaches, green beans, tomatoes, jellies, and jams that Jane put up will be welcome fare.

By the end of the season, the shelves in the cellar are crowded with jars of preserves and the freezer is packed with beef and about seventy bags of sweetcorn. Except when the chickens are moulting, the Steidingers will be assured of eggs, and, with a herd of dairy cows just outside the door, there's always plenty of milk.

The amount Jane cans seems large, but the jars, including these of peaches, will be empty and ready for filling all over again next summer.

Phil balances himself on the wagon pulled behind the baler while Mark drives the tractor. The hay has been cut and raked into windrows that circle the field. They work until sunset to get the hay in.

To get the farm animals stocked for the winter, Dennis buys straw from a neighbor's field. After the neighbor has harvested his wheat, Phil and Mark rake the leftover straw into rows. Next they use a tractor to pull the baler, a machine that picks up straw, molds and binds it with wire into tight bales. As the bales pound up the chute at the back of the baler, Phil stacks them on the wagon pulled behind the machine. The glistening straw is stored in the barn loft to be used for bedding to keep the cows warm and comfortable through the cold months.

The boys also bale hay, storing a blend of sweet clover and alfalfa in the loft of their barn. Over the summer there is a first, second, third, and occasionally a fourth cutting of hay. Each cutting produces more succulent hay than the last, but all of the crop will help feed the dairy herd through the winter. Toward summer's end, while still green, the cornfield out back is also cut and chopped for silage.

Both straw and hay must be baled during clear afternoons when the dew has dried. Wet straw or hay will get moldy, and if it rains during this time the crop will be ruined.

The Steidingers get about 3,500 bales of alfalfa from their fields and usually buy some extra hay to get them through the year.

Like her older brothers, ten-year-old Hope is responsible for many jobs around the farm. Every morning she feeds and waters their flock of leghorn chickens, then she and Mark take turns gathering the chalky, white eggs. The eggs aren't sold, but the chickens usually supply all the eggs the family needs. Hope also does the dishes, looks after her little sister, works in the garden, and waters the greenhouse plants. Yet it's not all work; Hope still finds time to jump on the backyard trampoline, pick flowers, or just play.

Hope feeds the chickens while she and Mark take turns collecting eggs. She also babysits Faith and generally helps out around the farm. "Sometimes chores are fun, sometimes they're not," she says. "I don't really like them too much, but they have to be done."

Despite the heat and monotony of walking beans, Dennis says, "It's still a good time for us. We have an opportunity to be together and talk."

Every season brings different chores. Through the winter months the fields lay dormant under a blanket of snow, but in the spring, they are plowed, raked smooth, and planted. In the summer, the rows of corn and soybeans are weeded with a cultivator pulled behind the tractor. During the autumn, the crops are harvested with a machine called a combine.

During the summer, just about all the family members must "walk beans," yanking large weeds with colorful names like smartweed, butterprint, and milkweed that were missed by the cultivator. If they aren't pulled, the weeds will jam the combine.

Walking beans is a hot, unwelcome summer ritual wherever the crop is grown. Each member of the crew—Dennis, Joy, Mark, and Hope—takes several rows. Once they get done with this chore, which takes one or two long mornings, the crew sometimes spends the rest of the afternoon cooling off at the swimming pool in town.

Dennis's grandfather, a German immigrant, first worked in this very same field when he settled on the farm in 1912. At that time Dennis's father was six years old. Later, Dennis was born on the farm. Jane came to the farm when she and Dennis married, and all of their eight children were born there. With Phil gradually assuming responsibility for the dairy herd, the Steidingers are now entering their fourth generation on their family farm.

Farms that have been in one family for at least a hundred years are often referred to as "centennial farms." The family farm is a source of pride and homes like the Steidingers' are always well cared for.

Field corn needs eight to ten inches of rain during the growing season (roughly mid-May to mid-October), and daily temperatures of at least seventy to eighty degrees Fahrenheit in July. It's then harvested by a combine that picks and shells the ears as the machine moves down the rows.

Because of the risk and large amount of work, the Steidingers once considered giving up their dairy operation in the late 1960s. Dennis's parents wrote to him about it while he was serving as a medic in Vietnam.

"I wrote back telling them not to sell the herd," Dennis recalls, "and it was the right decision." When he returned from the war he took over the dairy herd and, although he has always been keenly interested in horticulture, he's glad he kept the cows.

Even on a prudently managed farm like the Steidingers' uncertainties abound, not only from market prices, but also from the weather. Farmers need not only the right amount of rain, but it has to come at the right times. Crops must have rain just after planting and at regular intervals through the growing season, most critically in midsummer during pollination.

This past spring there was plenty of moisture in the ground when the Steidingers put in their corn and soybeans, and the hayfield was doing well, too. By midsummer, however, farmers in the Corn Belt, including the Steidingers, encountered a stretch of dry weather. "We sure could use some rain," Jane commented, her face wrinkling around the eyes as she glanced toward the sky. The grass in the yard had faded to brown and the tapered leaves of the corn had begun to crinkle at the edges.

Silage corn is harvested in late August or early September before the ears have fully matured. Silage corn is cut, chopped, and blown into a wagon. Here Dennis is harvesting silage.

Dennis worries until he gets into the fields to harvest his corn. The size of the silage crop depends upon a variety of factors, mostly the weather and damage from pests such as rootworms. If a crop is lost, the family would have to go into debt to purchase silage for feed.

"It's real bad over by Piper City—worse than here," Matt said. "The corn's starting to dry up."

Eventually, three-tenths of an inch of rain fell in a light drizzle over the fields. Dennis was glad for the rain, but quickly added, "We need at least a good half inch. The beans look all right, considering how dry it is, but the corn's pretty stressed."

Finally, in early August, the rain came—a good soaker—and the Steidingers relaxed a little. It wouldn't hurt if they got more rain between then and harvest, but that one steady downpour was critical. Again, they looked forward hopefully to a successful year, as they have every summer over the generations they have lived on the farm.

Because of sound management and the help of the family members, the Steidingers are able to make a go of their farm, while across the country family farms are vanishing from the rural landscape. From 1900 to 1990, the number of American farms has declined from more than five million to less than half that number. At the turn of the century, nearly thirty million people, more than 40 percent of the country's population, were farmers. By 1990, less than 2 percent of Americans lived on farms.

	Farm population (thousands)	Percentage of total population	Number of farms (thousands)	Acres in farms (thousands)	Average farm size (acres)
1900	29,875	41.9	5,740	841,202	147
1910	32,077	34.9	6,366	881,431	139
1920	31,974	30.1	6,454	958,677	149
1930	30,529	24.9	6,295	990,112	157
1940	30,547	23.2	6,102	1,065,114	175
1950	23,048	15.3	5,388	1,161,420	216
1960	15,635	8.7	3,962	1,175,646	297
1970	9,712	4.8	2,954	1,102,769	373
1980	6,051	2.7	2,439	1,038,885	426
1990	4,591	1.9	2,140	987,420	461

(*Sources:* Historical Statistics of the United States: Colonial times to 1970, *and the National Agricultural Statistics Service*)

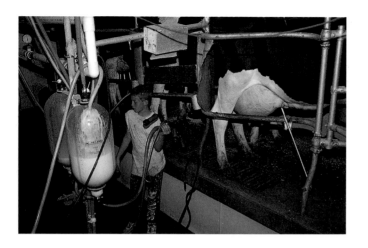

Jane and Dennis have raised each of their children to take care of the farm—and themselves. Although he just turned thirteen, Mark often handles the evening milking by himself.

For many years farmers were advised by agricultural leaders to be concerned only with markets and profits. Recently, however, an increasing number are returning to the conviction that farming is a way of life as well as a means of earning a livelihood. They believe that agriculture should be concerned about people as well as products. At one time, farmers assumed that soil erosion and chemical pollution of groundwater were necessary tradeoffs in agriculture. Now a growing number of men and women are practicing what is called "sustainable agriculture" to conserve the soil and to protect the environment for future generations.

By carefully managing each and every one of the resources on their farm — land, crops, livestock, buildings, equipment, and supplies — the Steidingers are making a go of their farm.

In the face of all difficulties, the family tradition survives. Matt is about to leave home to attend a university where he plans to study veterinary medicine. "I've always liked animals and have enjoyed caring for them," Matt says. "That's why I went into vet work."

Newly married to Jason Kilgus, a local dairyman, Joy is starting her life on another family farm. Joy says, "When I was growing up I didn't like living in the country, especially the winter months and the unpredictable mealtimes during harvest. But after graduation from high school and working in the city, I found the country life was really what I liked."

Many farmers have started organic farms to protect their land and to provide grain, produce, meat, eggs, and other non-treated foods to worried consumers. Many are also becoming concerned with preserving the quality of life for people in rural America. Larger farms not only reduce the number of farms, but also displace or impoverish many rural people. The large farms rely more heavily on migrant workers who work long hours for low wages. When they can no longer find jobs on farms or in areas related to agriculture, people must either move to a city or get by on marginal earnings. Today, 30 percent of the poor in America live in rural areas, and the number continues to grow each year.

Perhaps Dennis and Jane Steidinger's best work has been in raising their eight children, all of whom are or will be prepared to take a responsible place in the world. Having moved off the farm, Mike has gone to school to study horticulture. He helps his father with the greenhouse and works as a machinist at a tool and die shop. Matt will be going to college in the fall to study veterinary medicine. Tim isn't yet certain what he wants to do, but he, Mark, Hope, and Faith are learning the value of work and responsibility.

Whether working or enjoying a quiet moment, the Steidingers are always together on the farm. Here, Jane, Hope, and Faith are picking a few flowers for the table.

Having risen before dawn and worked all day, the Steidingers look forward to the evening. "Nothing compares with the quiet— a clear night, a full moon," Dennis says. "What I like most is the peacefulness here. I wouldn't trade it for anything."

"It's the inner satisfaction for me," Jane says, "of living close to God's creation."

It is uncertain just how many people will be able to continue farming the land in the future. Like many farm families, the Steidingers must confront the uncertainties of weather, luck, and economics. Yet they have an abiding faith that is strengthened every time a meal is placed on the table, every time a veil of rain descends on their dry fields, and every time a calf is born out there in the barn.

FURTHER READING

Excellent articles about farms may be found in the *World Book Encyclopedia* and the *Encyclopedia Americana,* both of which were consulted in the preparation of this book.

Statistical information was drawn from the 1993 edition of *Agricultural Statistics,* published by the Government Printing Office, Washington, D.C.

A number of books about farming are also available in libraries and bookstores for those who would like to read more about the family farm. The following books were helpful in the preparation of *Portrait of a Farm Family:*

Comstock, Gary, ed. *Is There a Moral Obligation to Save the Family Farm?* Ames, Iowa: Iowa State University Press, 1987.

Demisse, Ejigou. *Small-Scale Agriculture in America.* Boulder, Colo.: Westview Press, 1990.

Hurt, R. Douglas. *American Agriculture: A Brief History.* Ames, Iowa: Iowa State University Press, 1994.

Kline, David. *Great Possessions: An Amish Farmer's Journal.* San Francisco: North Point Press, 1990.

MacFadyen, J. Tevere. *Gaining Ground: The Renewal of America's Small Farms.* New York: Holt, Rinehart and Winston, 1984.

Paulsen, Gary. *Farm: A History and Celebration of the American Farmer.* Englewood Cliffs, N.J.: Prentice-Hall, Inc., 1977.

Rhodes, Richard. *Farm: A Year in the Life of an American Farmer.* New York: Simon and Schuster, 1989.

Rosenblatt, Paul C. *Farming Is in Our Blood.* Ames, Iowa: Iowa State University Press, 1990.

Strange, Marty. *Family Farming: A New Economic Vision.* Lincoln, Nebr.: University of Nebraska Press, 1988.

Wojcik, Jan. *The Arguments of Agriculture: A Casebook in Contemporary Agricultural Controversy.* West Lafayette, Ind.: ,.Purdue University Press, 1989.

Readers may also enjoy the following photoessays: *The Strength of the Hills: A Portrait of a Family Farm,* by Nancy Price Graff; *The American Family Farm: A Photoessay,* by Joan Anderson and George Ancona; and *Too Wet to Plow: the Family Farm in Transition,* by Jeanne Simonelli and Charles Winters.